-Party-
GAMES

Devised and illustrated by

Clare Beaton

Kingfisher Books

CONTENTS

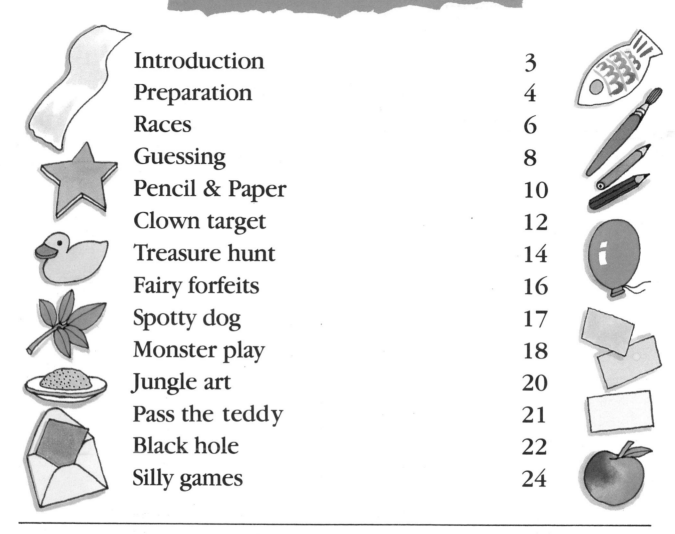

Produced by Times Four Publishing Ltd
Art and editorial direction: Tony Potter
Copy editor: Nicola Wright

Kingfisher Books, Grisewood & Dempsey Ltd,
Elsley House, 24-30 Great Titchfield St, London W1P 7AD

First published in 1991 by Kingfisher Books

10 9 8 7 6 5 4 3 2 1

Colour separations by RCS Graphics, Leeds
Typeset by C-Type, Horley, Surrey
Printed in Spain

BRITISH LIBRARY CATALOGUING IN PUBLICATION DATA
Beaton, Clare
    Children's party games.
    1. Games. Party. Children's
    I. Title   II. Series
    793.21

ISBN 0-86272-703-0

INTRODUCTION

Games are perhaps the most essential element of any children's party. This book is full of all sorts of different games - some you will recognize as variations on traditional favourites, while others involve you and the children in making novel props for games based on a theme, such as a 'black hole' for a space party.

Children need to release their energy running and jumping around, so there are plenty of races and musical games to choose from. Make sure you have enough space cleared indoors if you can't hold the party outdoors.

It's a good idea to intersperse these energetic games with quieter activities. You'll find the pencil and paper games, and guessing games, explained in the book are popular. Children also enjoy making or drawing things, especially if they can then use them afterwards in a game.

Some of the games are more suitable for younger children - some for older ones. Though most can be adapted for any age group as the basic rules are very simple. Many of the games are more fun when played in teams, especially if the number of guests is large.

PREPARATION

Be well prepared before the day of the party. It's a good idea to enlist some extra adult help on the day to set up each game in advance, so you avoid delays between games when children may get restless. Keep an eye on the time; starting off the party with games, serving tea in the middle, then having time for more games afterwards. If the weather permits, hold games outside for the space. If you are holding a party indoors, move furniture to the sides of your largest room and move anything breakable.

VARIETY

Try and alternate energetic, noisy games with quieter ones. However, if a game is particularly enjoyed and doesn't require a lot of setting up, for example races or musical bumps, don't be worried about repeating it. It may be a good idea to have some 'sitting down' games straight after tea so the children don't feel sick rushing around!

PLAN

Make a list of all the games you intend playing, in the order you intend to play them. Then split the list into two - the first half for games to play before tea, and the other half for after tea. Always have more games planned than you think you will need as it's difficult to judge how long each one will take. It is a good idea to try out any new games beforehand to ensure they will work.

GAMES TO PLAY
1. Jungle art
2. Spotty dog
3. Pass the teddy
4. Black hole
5. Treasure hunt
6. Guessing game
7. Forfeits

RULES

Whatever games you play, keep the rules simple and explain them clearly at the beginning. Take into account the age and sex of the party guests when deciding on the games. Whatever you decide, little boys and girls can be very determined if they decide they don't want to play a certain game!

JOINING IN

You often find that there's one child who feels too shy at first to join in with the others. Get them involved by asking them to help organize things to start with. Be careful about incorporating too many games where some people will have to 'sit out' as some children may get upset or become bored.

MUSIC

Make sure you have some music organized for your party. Children love to dance and jump around to popular tunes and many party games need music to play them properly. You can buy special party tapes for children, or you could make your own from the radio or records. Have someone in charge of the music.

PROPS

Have all your props together in a box - music tapes, small prizes, stop watch, and so on. You can make some of these beforehand with your child. Masks or badges are simple to make and you can suit them to a theme if you are having one.

PRIZES

Children enjoy winning prizes, but they needn't be expensive. Toy shops are full of little novelties, such as miniature packs of cards and bits of stationery. Small boxes of crayons are also popular. Try to avoid giving out too many sweets, especially before tea.

Pass the parcel is always a popular game to play. Rather than having just one prize in the centre, you could place a few little ones between other layers.

Crayons

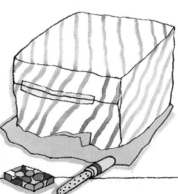

Rather than just giving a prize to the winner of a game, have some games where a team, or everyone taking part, wins something. If you are giving out prizes, it might be a good idea to put them in the 'going home' bags so the children can easily find them later to take home.

Badges or small toys

Emma

RACES

Races are better held outdoors, though some can be held indoors if the room is big enough. Clear away as much furniture as possible to the sides of the room and move anything breakable!

THREE-LEGGED

Divide the party guests into pairs and tie them together by the ankle (not too tightly) using old ties or rope. Hold relay races in teams.

WHEELBARROW

A wheelbarrow race is run in pairs. One person gets down on all fours, while their partner picks them up by their ankles. When everyone is ready in this position, they set off for the finish line - trying not to collapse!

RED ROVER

The more players you have for *Red Rover* the better. Everyone lines up on one side of the room or garden. One person is chosen to stand alone, some distance from the line. When he or she shouts "Red Rover all over", everyone must run over to the other side while the caller tries to catch someone. Whoever is caught joins the caller as the others run back the other way. Together they try and catch more people. Whoever is the last to be caught is the winner.

EGG & SPOON

Don't play this rather messy game indoors! Everyone lines up holding a spoon with an egg balanced in it. Whoever makes it to the finish line with their egg still intact on their spoon wins.

SACK RACE

Hessian sacks are the best to use for a sack race, though bin liners, potato sacks or old pillow cases are more easily available. Have a start and finish line. The best technique is to jump with both feet together, holding the sack with both hands!

Old pillow case

Plastic bin liner

FINISH

STEPPING STONES

Stepping stones is a simple but fun game. All you need are two sheets of paper per player. As each player steps forward, they must place a sheet of paper in front for their foot to step on to. Before they can step forward again they must lift up their back foot, pick up the piece of paper, and balance on one foot while placing the paper in front again. It's not as easy as it sounds, especially if you make it a team race!

MEDALS

The birthday child can help to make these medals to give to the winners of races and team relays.

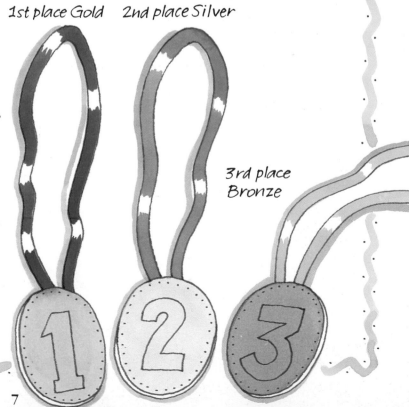

1st place Gold   2nd place Silver

3rd place Bronze

Cut circles out of thick silver, gold and bronze coloured card.

Cut lengths of ribbon and tape the ends to the back of each medal.

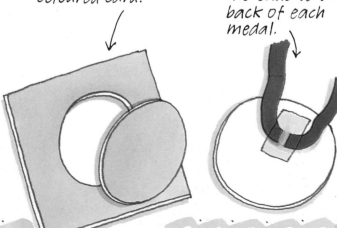

GUESSING

GUESS WHAT SMELL

Guessing games are always popular and make good competitions. To play *Guess what smell* you will need a blindfold and a number of 'smelly' items. Make some difficult, for example, a slice of bread, washing up liquid - and some easy, for example, a rose or coffee. Each player has one guess per item, for which they get one point if it's correct. Whoever gets the most points is the winner.

GUESS WHAT TASTE

This game is also played with a blindfold and involves guessing what things are by tasting them. Avoid too many strong tasting foods or players will feel sick! Try out sugar, salt, custard and cocoa powder. To make guessing more difficult, try various flavours of crisps or jams.

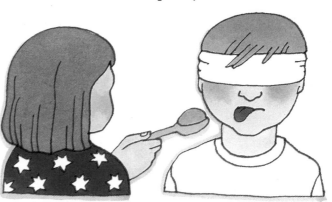

SQUEAK, PIGGY, SQUEAK

For this game, one person is blindfolded while the others sit around the room, preferably in soft chairs or on cushions. Whoever is blindfolded walks around the room and then sits down on someone's lap, saying "Squeak, piggy, squeak". Whoever they are sitting on starts squeaking, and the blindfolded person must try to guess the identity of the squeaker. If the guess is correct, the squeaker becomes the person to be blindfolded.

GUESS WHO

Guess who is played in pairs. The organizer writes down the names of famous people or types of animals on bits of paper and then pins one to the back of each player. One member of the pair then looks at the label on their partner's back and mimes that person or animal until the partner guesses who they are. They mustn't give spoken clues.

COW

Ideas:

Cow   Bird

Dog   Cat

Horse

Ideas:

Michael Jackson

The Queen

E.T.

Madonna

GUESS WHAT

You will need . . .

Cardboard box
Coloured wrapping
paper
Small household
objects

Cover a cardboard
box with colourful
wrapping paper.

Place the objects to
be guessed inside.

Cut out two holes
in each side of the
box, big enough for
a child's hand to fit
through.

Players take it in turns to feel the objects in the
box, writing down their guesses as they go along.
You could set a time limit to make it harder.
When everyone has had their turn, open the box
and check the lists to find out who got the most
guesses correct.

What objects you decide to put in the box will
depend on the age group of the children at the
party. Make most of them household items -
some hard and some easy.

For younger children you could use
a rubber duck, orange, toy car,
comb, teddy bear and sponge.

For older children you can have
more difficult objects. For example,
a woolly hat, playing card, paper clip, banana,
tube of toothpaste, pair of sunglasses,
sandpaper, roll of sticky tape.

PENCIL & PAPER

Party games tend to be noisy when there are lots of children, so it may be a good idea to include some quieter, less energetic games. This gives the organizers, and the guests, a rest! For most of the following games all you need to provide are pencils and paper.

LONG WORDS

To play this game you need to think of a long word, such as 'nightingale'. Players then have five minutes to write down all the words they can make out of 'nightingale', for example, 'night', 'gale', 'nail', 'gate' and so on. They must not be proper names. Count up the words. The winner is the person who has most words on their list.

LAST LETTERS

You can have any number of players for this game. Everyone sits in a circle. One person calls out the name of something. It can be a country, an animal, a vegetable or a flower. If 'daffodil' is called out, the other players must write it down and then try to think of a flower beginning with the last letter, for example, 'lilac'. Then a flower beginning with the letter 'c', and so on until everyone gets stuck. Count up each player's list of words. The winner is the one with the most words. With older children, you could play this game without writing the words down, just saying them out loud.

PICTURE WORDS

This is an amusing team game. Each person writes down the name of an object on a separate strip of paper, folds it up and places it in a hat or bag. A member from one team picks out a piece of paper and looks at the word. He or she then has one minute to draw the word. The other team members must try to guess what the word is. If they guess the word before the time is up, the team wins a point. Each team should have the same number of turns and the one with the most points at the end wins.

HEADS & BODIES

Heads and bodies is a drawing
game which can produce
hilarious results. Each player
draws a hat at the top of a
long piece of paper, and then folds it back along
the bottom edge of the drawing. Everyone then
hands their paper to the person on their left
who draws a head and neck. Again everyone folds
the paper back, this time so that only the
bottom of the neck can be seen, and passes
it on. This continues for the body,
the legs and finally the feet. The
papers are folded over for
the last time and passed
on. Unfold them for
a surprise!

Fold
over
here.

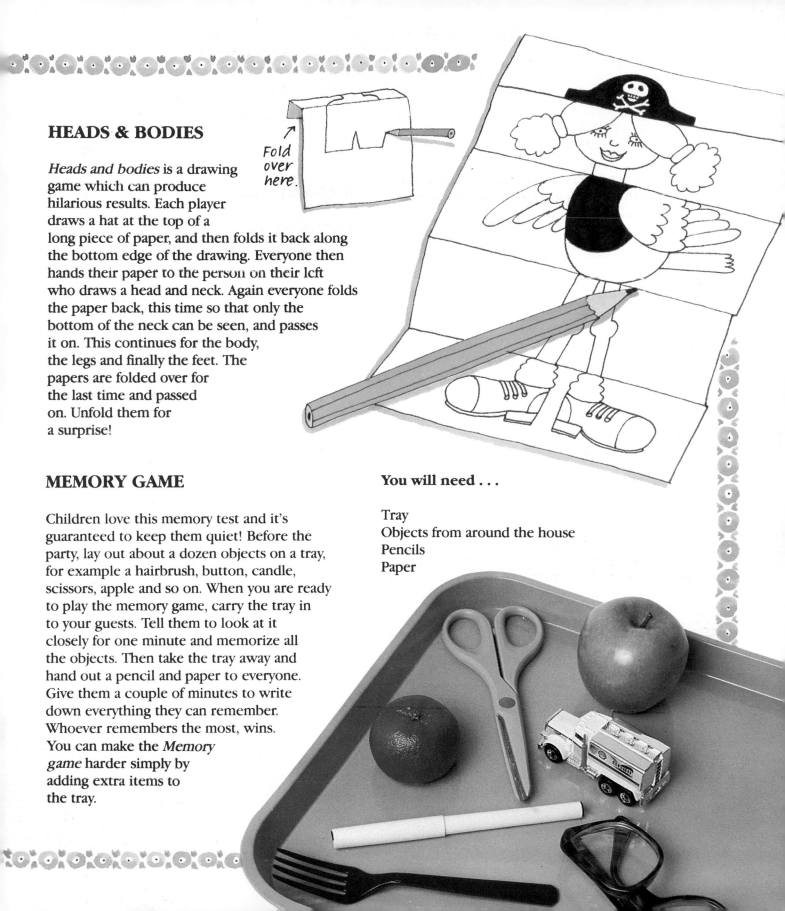

MEMORY GAME

Children love this memory test and it's
guaranteed to keep them quiet! Before the
party, lay out about a dozen objects on a tray,
for example a hairbrush, button, candle,
scissors, apple and so on. When you are ready
to play the memory game, carry the tray in
to your guests. Tell them to look at it
closely for one minute and memorize all
the objects. Then take the tray away and
hand out a pencil and paper to everyone.
Give them a couple of minutes to write
down everything they can remember.
Whoever remembers the most, wins.
You can make the *Memory
game* harder simply by
adding extra items to
the tray.

You will need . . .

Tray
Objects from around the house
Pencils
Paper

CLOWN TARGET

Children will enjoy helping to make these targets as well as playing the game. The clown's face shown here was created with a circus theme in mind, though you could make a spaceman's head for a space party, and so on. This game is not recommended for younger children.

You will need . . .

Coloured card
Tissue paper
Scissors
Glue
Cocktail sticks
Blu-tack
Large straws

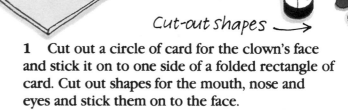

Fold here

Glue stick

Cut-out shapes

1 Cut out a circle of card for the clown's face and stick it on to one side of a folded rectangle of card. Cut out shapes for the mouth, nose and eyes and stick them on to the face.

Cut out mouth

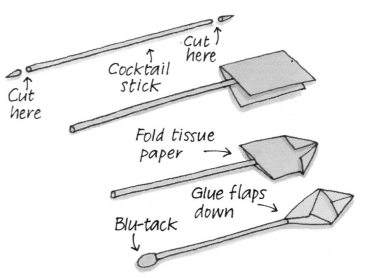

Cut here

Cut here

Cocktail stick

Fold tissue paper

Blu-tack

Glue flaps down

2 With a pencil, draw a line inside the mouth shape, leaving enough space to look like lips. Carefully cut out the rest of the mouth with a craft knife to leave a large hole.

3 To make the 'arrows', cut the sharp ends off cocktail sticks. Then stick a small blob of Blu-tack on one end and a tissue paper diamond-shaped 'tail' on the other end.

To fire . . .

Place the arrow, Blu-tack end first, down a straw, then blow hard down the straw, aiming to shoot the arrow through the clown's mouth.

Scoring

Make three arrows for each child and give points for direct hits. You could make a target for each child if numbers were small. Alternatively, make a couple of targets and hold competitions between teams.

WARNING: Do not let children aim at each other.

Ideas for other targets.

Younger children could flip tiddlywinks into the clown's mouth, or throw Smarties from a marked distance.

CLOWN BALLOONS

Get the children to decorate balloons with clowns' faces. Draw a face using felt-tips or cut out shapes for eyes, nose and mouth from paper and stick on to a blown-up balloon. A good balloon game involves everyone standing in a line and passing the balloon, without using their hands, from one end of the line to the other. Play the game in teams. If someone drops the balloon it must go back to the beginning of the line again.

You could decorate balloons to suit other party themes.

TREASURE HUNT

Treasure hunts are always popular with children, but you do need to prepare well before the party. Outdoors is the best place to hold a treasure hunt, especially if there are lots of participants, although clues could also be hidden indoors if there is enough space. Dividing the children into teams is more fun and more successful than playing individually.

Differently-coloured envelopes for each team.

You will need . . .

Pencil
Paper
Envelopes
Treasure

Depending on the number of children playing, divide them into at least two teams - Team 1, Team 2, and so on. The organizer then works out approximately ten different hiding places for clues. For example, if the hiding place is under a wheelbarrow, the clue for it could say 'The next hiding place is under something used for wheeling things round the garden'.

There should be a copy of each clue for every team. The last clue should lead the teams to the treasure, which the organizer hides before the start of the game. The treasure could be sweets or little toys. If you are having a theme party you could hide something appropriate, for example, chocolate coins at a pirate party.

Put each clue in a different envelope, marked with the number of each team, and leave them in the hiding places, apart from the first clue which should be handed out at the start. To avoid one team just following another to each hiding place, try and place each team's clues in a different order. The winning team is the one that finds the treasure first.

HUNT THE PUZZLE

Old birthday card

Cut up old birthday or Christmas cards to make puzzles. One for each child or team. Or you could stick pictures from magazines onto thin card and cut up. Strong, clear images work best. Hide the pieces separately around the house. The winner is the one who completes their puzzle first.

Cut into several large pieces.

FIND THE BURIED TREASURE

Younger children may find clues hard to follow, so you could try this buried treasure hunt instead:

You will need . . .

Paints or pens   Thin polystyrene sheet
Papers   Cocktail sticks
Scissors   Treasure

Draw a tropical island scene on a large piece of paper. Then cut around the island, leaving the top edge uncut so that it can be lifted up. Place the paper over polystyrene and, without the children seeing, mark an X on the polystyrene under the island. Each child must guess where the treasure is buried on the island by sticking in a flag (made from a cocktail stick and paper). Lift the island up to see whose flag is nearest the X. The winner is awarded the treasure.

NATURE HUNT

Paper or plastic bag

A nature hunt is a good idea if you can play in a park or garden. Give each child a list of things to find, some easy, some more difficult. Here are some ideas:

Twig
Leaves (various)
Stone
Feather
Flower (various)
Piece of litter
Seed

FAIRY FORFEITS

This forfeit game can be adapted to any party with a theme. This version has a fairy theme, so instructions are given to show you how to make a wand pointer board and lily pads with different forfeits written on the back. The rules are simple - each child sits on his or her own lily pad in a circle and takes turns in spinning the pointer. Whoever it points to when it stops has to turn over their lily pad and perform the forfeit. When they have finished they can sit out. The last person left in is the winner.

Forfeit suggestions:

- You have been turned into a frog - jump up and down 10 times.
- Run around the circle singing 'Ring-a-ring-of-roses.'
- Pat your head with one hand and rub your stomach with your other hand at the same time.

Lily pad

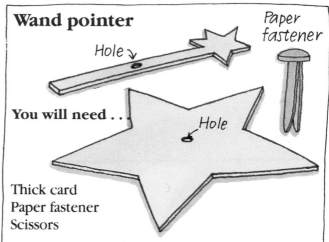

Wand pointer

Hole

Paper fastener

Hole

You will need . . .

Thick card
Paper fastener
Scissors

Cut a giant star shape out of the card for the board. Then cut out a smaller star and a long strip (for the shaft of the wand). Make a hole in the middle of the wand and the board. Place a paper fastener through the holes, flattening out the prongs at the back. Don't secure it too tightly or the wand won't spin.

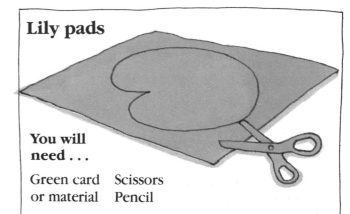

Lily pads

You will need . . .

Green card   Scissors
or material   Pencil

Draw a simple lily pad shape in pencil and trace it on to the green card or material, making one for each guest. Cut out the shapes. Then write a forfeit on the back of each pad (if using material, write the forfeits on paper and tape them on).

SPOTTY DOG

You will need . . .

Large piece of paper
Lots of small circles
of black paper or
sticky spots.

Pen or pencil
Blu-tack

For this game, you need to draw the basic outline of a dog and pin it to a wall. Divide the dog's body into areas, each scoring different points. Then stick a blob of Blu-tack to one side of the small circles of black paper. Each child is blindfolded and when it is their turn they are given several spots which they try to stick on the dog. If they miss altogether they get no points. At the end of each round add up the points to see who has scored the most.

MUSICAL SPOTS

With a 'spotty' theme in mind, try musical spots as a variation on musical chairs or bumps.

You will need . . .

Card, paper or material
Pen or pencil

Round object
Music

Use a large circular object to draw around on your card or material. Cut out one 'spot' for each guest and place them in the centre of the room. Play some music so the children can dance around the spots. When it stops they must sit down on a spot or they are out. Remove one more spot each time. Whoever sits on the last spot has won.

MONSTER PLAY

Children love to make things, so why not let their imaginations run riot making a monster! You could divide the children into teams and hold a competition to see who can make the best monster. It might be a good way to start a party by getting everyone involved. Start collecting suitable materials well in advance. The following items would make good basics which you can add to depending on what you have around the house.

Cartons

Cardboard tubes ↘

Silver foil

Yoghurt pots

Coloured paper

Glue

Newspaper

Felt pens

Paints

Wool

String

This is an activity that could be adapted to other party themes. For example, you could get the children to make an astronaut or a rocket at a space party.

MONSTER STATUES

For this game, children simply move around the room 'monster-fashion' to music, making suitable monster noises! When the music stops they must hold whatever position they are in for several seconds until the music starts again. Anyone who moves has to sit out. This is a game that could be adapted to other themes. At a jungle party, each child could pick an animal to imitate.

WHAT'S THE TIME, MIGHTY MONSTER?

Replace the traditional Mr Wolf character of this game with an equally menacing Mighty Monster. The more players you have, the more fun the game is. Whoever is chosen as Mighty Monster starts walking away from the rest of the players, who then start following him or her. Everyone together asks loudly "What's the time, Mighty Monster?". The monster can say any time it likes, but when the answer is "12 o'clock, dinner time", everyone must run back to the start. Mighty Monster runs after them and whoever is caught, or is last home, becomes the next Mighty Monster.

JUNGLE ART

Children love being able to create their own pictures, especially on a giant scale. Friezes and collages are often a good way of starting a party by getting the children involved from the moment they arrive. Some won't want to tear themselves away!

You will need . . .
Rolls of old wallpaper
Magazines
Coloured paper
Pens or crayons
Scissors and glue
Sticky tape or drawing pins

You don't have to be an artist to start off a frieze. Just pin or tape wallpaper to the walls in strips and draw very basic outlines. The children will do the rest.

For a collage, it may be a good idea to cut out some shapes ready for sticking and colouring in or for drawing round.

Ideas for collage shapes

Children will enjoy drawing around each other posing in different positions. Make sure they don't draw too close to the person or it will mark their clothes.

Colour in the outlines in felt-tip pen or crayon.

PASS THE TEDDY

To play *Pass the teddy*, the children must stand in a circle. Start playing some music and give a teddy bear to one child. He or she then passes it to their left and so on around the circle, from person to person. When the music stops, whoever is holding the teddy bear is out. The last person left holding the teddy is the winner.

TEAM TEDDIES

Team teddies is a more difficult version of *Pass the teddy* involving more skill and more teddies! The children divide into two teams and stand in a line. Someone says "Ready, teddy, go!" and they start trying to pass a number of teddies down the line using any part of their bodies except their hands. If a teddy touches the ground at all, it must go back to the beginning of the line again. Whichever team first manages to get all their teddies safely to the end of their line, wins a prize.

BLACK HOLE

Combining luck and skill, this game is a space variation of the traditional indoor fishing game using fishing rods and magnets.

You will need . . .

Coloured paper (silver and gold)
Paper clips
Scissors
Sticky tape
Magnet
String and garden cane
Dustbin or bucket
Black plastic sack

1   To create a 'black hole', line a bucket or dustbin with a black plastic sack. You could decorate the outside by sticking on cut-out stars, planets and rockets.

2   Using the coloured paper, cut out stars, moons, planets, spacemen and alien shapes. Instead of using silver paper, you could cover shapes with tin foil.

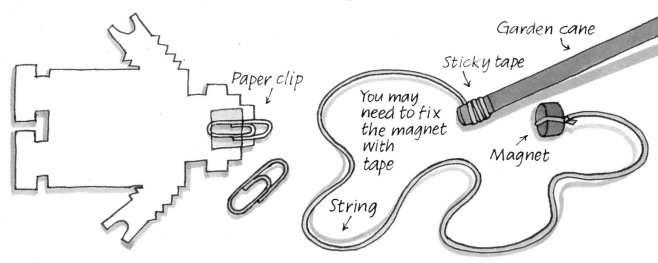

3   Attach a metal paper clip to the back of each shape using sticky tape, leaving enough metal exposed to attract the magnet. Place the shapes at the bottom of the 'black hole'.

4   To make the fishing rod, tie a piece of string to one end of a length of garden cane, securing it with sticky tape. Then tie a small magnet to the other end of the string.

VARIATIONS:

You could paint a cut-down cardboard box to make a chest.

Tape paper clips to chocolate coins and paper parrots.

Pirate

Use a basket or a wooden chest as a container. 'Fish' for chocolate coins and paper parrots.

Jungle

Decorate a cardboard box with green paper leaves and 'fish' for paper animals.

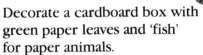

Paper leaves   Cardboard box

How to play . . .

You could hold team competitions, writing different points on the back of the different shapes to be 'fished' for. At the end of a time limit, add up each team's points to find the winners.

SILLY GAMES

There are some games that can only be described as 'silly', but children often find them the most fun!

SWINGING APPLES

This game is a race to see who can eat their apple the quickest. Use a metal skewer to make a hole through the centre of each apple. Then push a length of string through the hole and tie a knot. Hang up the apples at mouth height, then munch away!

SWEET BOBBING

This game will be very messy, so make sure you put down newspaper or an old sheet if playing it indoors. Put some sweets, such as marshmallows (avoid hard varieties that could choke children), on top of some flour or icing sugar in a bowl. The players take it in turns to kneel down and try to pick the sweets up without using their hands. Whoever manages to eat the most wins.

FLIP THE KIPPER

To make . . .

The idea of *Flip the kipper* is to race all the kippers. Let the children cut their own kippers out of crêpe or tissue paper. For easy recognition they could also colour the kippers in and draw on eyes, scales and fins.

To race . . .

Line the fish up side by side. To move the fish along, wave a folded newspaper up and down to create a breeze.